BIRDFEEDERS

Renée Schwarz

KIDS CAN PRESS

To my little chickadees: Sophie, Pippa and Alex

Kids Can Press acknowledges the financial support of the Government of Ontario, through the Ontario Media Development Corporation's Ontario Book Initiative, and the Government of Canada, through the BPIDP, for our publishing activity.

Published in Canada by
Kids Can Press Ltd.
29 Birch Avenue
Toronto, ON M4V 1E2

Published in the U.S. by
Kids Can Press Ltd.
2250 Military Road
Tonawanda, NY 14150

www.kidscanpress.com

Edited by Stacey Roderick
Designed by Kathleen Collett
Photography by Frank Baldassarra

Printed and bound in China

The hardcover edition of this book is smyth sewn casebound.
The paperback edition of this book is limp sewn with a drawn-on cover.

CM 05 0 9 8 7 6 5 4 3 2 1
CM PA 05 0 9 8 7 6 5 4 3 2 1

Library and Archives Canada Cataloguing in Publication Data

Schwarz, Renée
    Birdfeeders / Renée Schwarz.

(Kids can do it)
ISBN 1-55337-699-4 (bound).   ISBN 1-55337-700-1 (pbk.)

1. Bird feeders — Design and construction — Juvenile literature.
I. Title. II. Series.

QL676.5.S348 2005   j690'.8927   C2004-906027-9

Kids Can Press is a /orus™ Entertainment company

Contents

Introduction

Make a birdfeeder to hang in your backyard or on your balcony, and birds will come to eat where you can watch them. Make a few, and they may come in flocks.

All of these feeders can be made in an afternoon and will last for years. The skills you need to make them are easy to learn, even if you've never used some of the tools. Just be sure to ask an adult to help when drilling or sawing. And be sure to follow the safety tips.

The best thing about building birdfeeders is seeing the birds come to feed. Check the chart at the back of the book for favorite bird foods. Once birds are used to coming to your feeder, try standing very, very still with some seeds in your hand. You might get some birds, like chickadees, eating out of your hand!

MATERIALS AND TOOLS

Most of the materials and tools you will need are easily found in hardware stores. You might also find some of the things you'll use in the recycling bin. And look around your home for extra wooden boards, nails, screws and so on — but always ask first before you use anything.

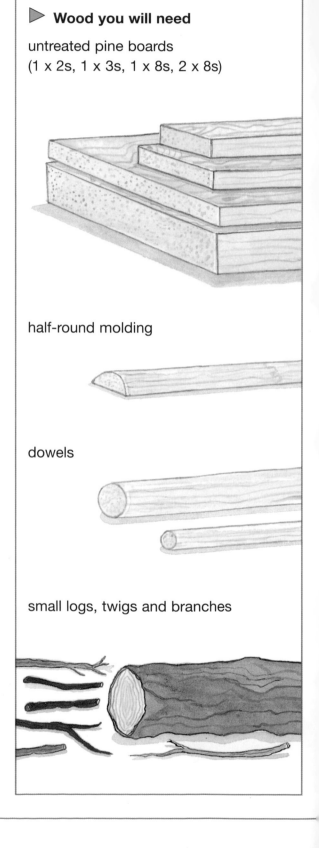

▷ **Wood you will need**

untreated pine boards
(1 x 2s, 1 x 3s, 1 x 8s, 2 x 8s)

half-round molding

dowels

small logs, twigs and branches

4

▷ **Other materials you will need for making and decorating the birdfeeders**

plastic bottles

tin can

tomato cage

plastic flowerpot and saucers

Frisbee

garden claw

plastic funnel

wall scraper

old metal tablespoon

plastic lids and tops

wooden beads and Popsicle sticks

scissors

pencils and rulers

oil pastel crayons and permanent markers

Safety notes:

★ Wear work gloves and safety glasses when working.

★ Ask an adult to help when sawing and drilling.

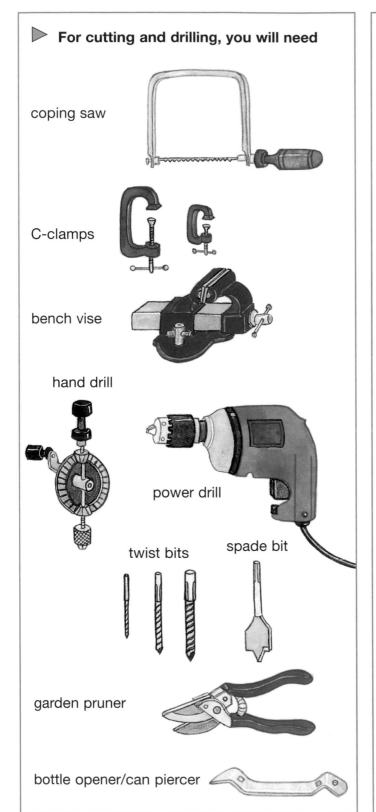

▶ For cutting and drilling, you will need

coping saw

C-clamps

bench vise

hand drill

power drill

twist bits spade bit

garden pruner

bottle opener/can piercer

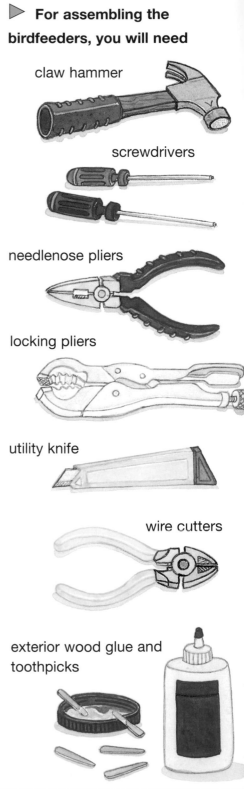

▶ For assembling the birdfeeders, you will need

claw hammer

screwdrivers

needlenose pliers

locking pliers

utility knife

wire cutters

exterior wood glue and toothpicks

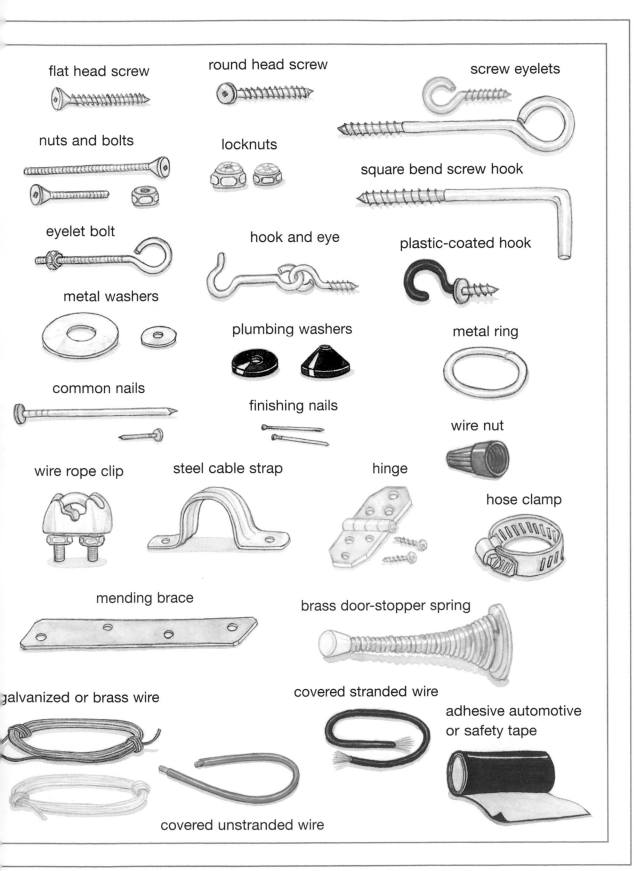

flat head screw

round head screw

screw eyelets

nuts and bolts

locknuts

square bend screw hook

eyelet bolt

hook and eye

plastic-coated hook

metal washers

plumbing washers

metal ring

common nails

finishing nails

wire nut

wire rope clip

steel cable strap

hinge

hose clamp

mending brace

brass door-stopper spring

galvanized or brass wire

covered stranded wire

adhesive automotive or safety tape

covered unstranded wire

Techniques

Read this section before starting any of the projects. Also ask an adult to work with you and show you how to use the tools.

Safety

Always wear work gloves and safety glasses to protect yourself, especially when drilling, sawing or working with wire. Always ask an adult to use the power drill.

Hand tools are safe when used carefully. Never force a tool, because it can slip and hurt you. Take your time. Read the instructions with an adult before starting a project. If something is difficult, ask an adult for help.

Work surface

A worktable or workbench is the best surface to use. Otherwise a large wooden board can be used instead.

Clamping

It is important to clamp the pieces to your work surface so they do not move when you are drilling or sawing.

Small or round things, like bottles, branches and bottle tops, are sometimes difficult to hold in a C-clamp or vise — ask an adult helper to hold them in place.

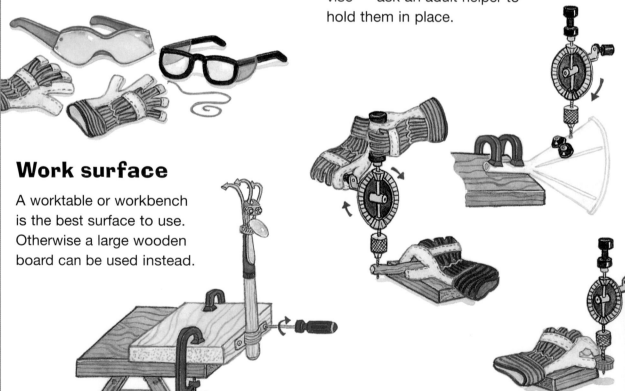

Sawing

Wear work gloves and safety glasses, and make sure the wood is firmly clamped in place.

Use a coping saw to cut molding and wooden shapes. For shapes, draw on the wood, clamp the wood in place and cut out the shape. Rather than sawing the whole shape with one cut, it is usually easier to start cutting at different points that meet.

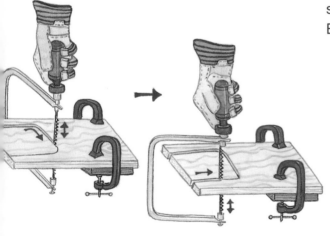

Drilling

Clamp the piece securely so it will not spin, or have someone carefully hold it in place. Make sure the part being drilled sticks out past your work surface or place a scrap piece of wood underneath so you don't drill into the work surface.

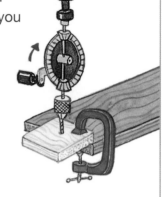

Wearing work gloves and safety glasses, use a hand drill to drill drainage holes and holes for perches and for drilling pilot (or starter) holes before nailing or screwing. Ask an adult to use a power drill with a spade bit for drilling the big holes in the Bird Dog.

Drilling tips:

* Do not push hard on the drill when drilling through plastic or the plastic might crack.

* Before nailing Popsicle sticks or branches, drill small pilot holes first so the wood doesn't split.

Screwing

Choose a screwdriver that fits in the slot on the head of the screw or bolt. The tip of the screwdriver should fit tightly so that it does not slip out when turned.

Screws, screw eyes, hooks, nuts and bolts always turn clockwise (to the right) to tighten and counterclockwise (to the left) to loosen. Just remember: "righty-tighty, lefty-loosey."

Locknuts

A locknut is a nut with an extra section that locks it in place. To screw one onto a bolt, grasp the nut in the locking pliers with one hand. With your other hand, screw in the bolt using a screwdriver. Since locknuts can be hard to screw on, you may need to ask an adult for help.

Wire

When using wire to hold or attach things, hook the end of the wire through both pieces. Then twist the wire end back around itself a few times to hold it in place. **Cut wire is sharp, so wear work gloves and safety glasses.**

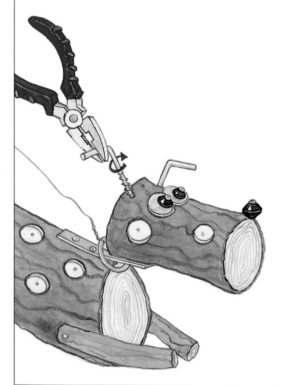

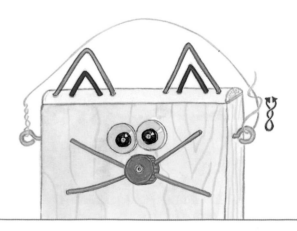

Tips for mounting and care

Hang or mount your birdfeeders on fence posts, in trees, on the clothesline or on a window ledge. Be patient! It may take the birds a few weeks to discover your feeder.

● Different birds like different foods. Check the chart at the back of the book for food ideas.

● Place the feeder where cats can't climb up or jump on it. If possible, place the feeder near some bushes so the birds can quickly fly there to hide.

● To keep squirrels off your feeder, either buy a squirrel baffle (available from most stores that sell bird food) or move the feeder to a spot squirrels can't reach. If that doesn't work, watching squirrels can also be fun.

● Wear rubber gloves to clean the feeder every few weeks with hot water. Scrub it with a brush to unclog the drainage holes so rainwater can drain out easily. Also check to see if anything needs to be fixed. Make sure that there are no sharp bits that can hurt the birds.

● **Do not suddenly stop feeding the birds.** Reduce the amount of food you put out gradually so the birds get used to looking elsewhere.

Mushroom

You'll find birds instead of a leprechaun under this toadstool!

You will need

- a clean, large juice can with one end removed
- 20 cm (8 in.) diameter plastic flowerpot saucer
- four 1/4 metal washers
- two 1 in. bolts and nuts
- 15 cm (6 in.) diameter plastic flowerpot
- red adhesive tape or red permanent marker
- two 40 cm (16 in.) lengths of 18 gauge galvanized or coated wire
- a metal ring
- pencil, marker, ruler and scissors
- work gloves and safety glasses
- bottle opener/can piercer, needlenose pliers, C-clamps, hand drill with a 1/4 in. bit and a 1/8 in. bit, screwdriver

1 Make two holes on the bottom of the juice can, as shown.

2 Around the outside of the can, make four holes near the bottom and two holes near the top, as shown. Squeeze any sharp edges flat with the pliers.

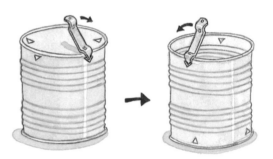

3 Stand the can in the saucer. With the marker, mark the two bottom holes on the saucer. Remove the can.

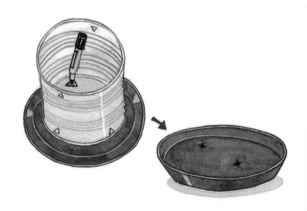

4 Clamp the saucer to your work surface and use the ¼ in. bit to drill the two holes that you marked in step 3. Also drill six drainage holes into the bottom, as shown.

5 Stand the can in the saucer so that the bottom holes line up. Slip a washer onto each bolt. Poke each bolt through a hole in the saucer and the can.

6 Slip a second washer onto each bolt and screw on a nut. Grasp the nut with the pliers and tighten the bolt with the screwdriver.

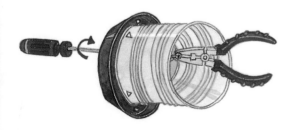

7 Clamp the flowerpot and drill two ⅛ in. holes in the bottom, about 4 cm (1½ in.) apart.

8 To decorate, cut circles out of the tape and stick them on the pot. Or draw spots on with the red marker.

9 Poke an end of each wire through a hole near the top of the can and twist it to hold. Poke each wire up through a hole in the bottom of the pot. Wind the ends of the wire around the metal ring and twist them to hold. Slide the pot down onto the can.

10 To fill the can with seeds, slide the pot up the wires.

Itsy bitsy spider

Rain or shine, birds will come to visit.

You will need

- a Frisbee or a large plastic saucer
- two black beveled plumbing washers
- two $1/2$ in. bolts and two nuts
- $1 1/2$ in. eyelet bolt and nut
- four 60 cm (24 in.) lengths of 12 gauge blue covered wire
- eight 40 cm (16 in.) lengths of 20 gauge galvanized wire
- a metal ring
- work gloves and safety glasses
- marker and ruler
- C-clamps, hand drill with a $9/64$ in. bit, screwdriver, pliers

1 Clamp the Frisbee (the spider's body) to your work surface. Drill a few holes into it for drainage, as shown.

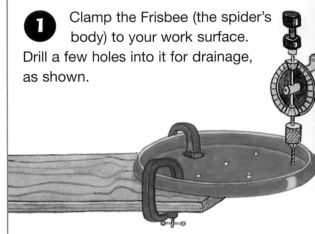

2 For the eyes, mark and drill two holes in the rim, about 2 cm ($3/4$ in.) apart.

3 Slip a black washer onto a $1/2$ in. bolt. Using the screwdriver, screw the bolt through an eye hole. Then screw a nut onto the end of the bolt. Repeat for the other eye.

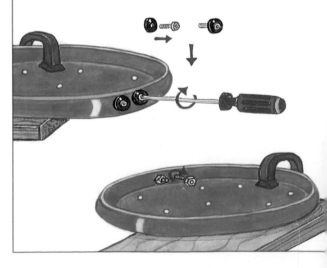

4 For the nose, drill a hole centered just below the eyes.

5 Screw the eyelet bolt through the nose hole. Then screw the nut onto the end of the bolt.

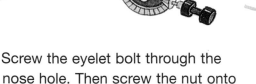

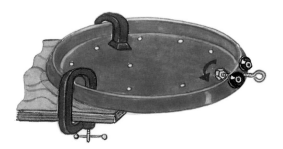

6 For the legs, mark and drill four holes on each side of the rim, about 8 cm (3 in.) apart.

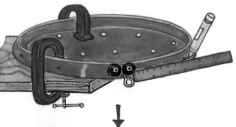

7 Poke a blue wire through one leg hole and out the next. Pull it through until the ends are even. Repeat three times to make eight legs.

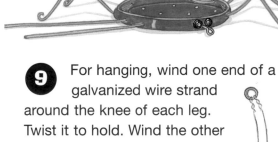

8 Make three bends in each leg: one upward bend near the Frisbee, another downward in the middle (the knee) and finally one up near the tip (the foot). Use pliers to bend the tip into a loop.

9 For hanging, wind one end of a galvanized wire strand around the knee of each leg. Twist it to hold. Wind the other end around the metal ring, twisting it to hold.

Other idea

• To make this into a birdbath, place a plastic dish filled with water inside the Frisbee.

Fruit flowers

These flowers bloom all year.

You will need

- 1 x 3 pine board, 6 cm (2½ in.) long
- a plastic peanut butter or mayonnaise jar lid, about 8 cm (3 in.) diameter
- eight Popsicle sticks
- exterior wood glue and a rag
- sixteen ½ in. nails   • ¼ metal washer
- $3/16$ x 1¼ in. bolt and locknut
- 30 cm (12 in.) length of 20 gauge brass wire
- half an orange
- two 1½ in. common nails   • oil pastel crayons
- pencil and ruler
- work gloves and safety glasses
- C-clamps, hand drill with a $1/16$ in. bit and a $3/16$ in. bit, wire cutters, hammer, locking pliers, screwdriver

1 Clamp the board to your work surface. Mark an X in the center and drill a $3/16$ in. hole through it.

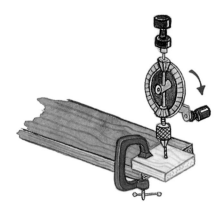

2 Clamp the plastic lid and drill a $3/16$ in. hole in the center. Also drill two holes on opposite sides of the rim, as shown.

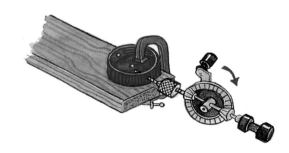

3 For the petals, carefully cut the Popsicle sticks in half with the wire cutters.

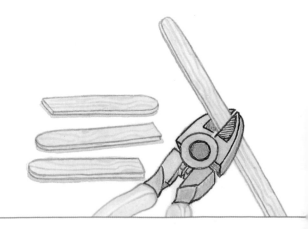

4 Drill $1/16$ in. pilot holes near the cut ends of the Popsicle sticks. Dab some glue on the back near the holes and nail them around the board using the $1/2$ in. nails. Wipe off excess glue.

5 Color the petals with pastels.

6 Slip the washer on the bolt. Poke the bolt through the hole in the center of the lid first and then through the hole in the center of the board. Screw the locknut onto the bolt (see page 10).

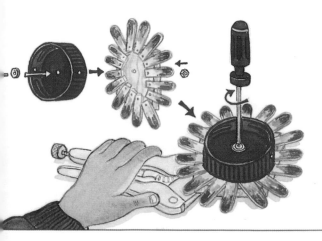

7 For hanging, bend the wire in half and slide it up between the lid and the petals so the bend catches on the bolt. Twist the wires together and make a loop near the end. Twist the ends back around the wire to hold the loop in place.

8 Place the half orange in the lid. Poke the $1 1/2$ in. nails through the side holes in the lid to hold the orange in place.

Other idea

• For a different treat, fill the lid with suet or peanut butter.

Feeder fly

A rather seedy character.

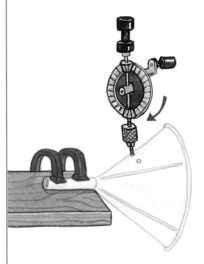

1 Clamp the funnel (the fly's head) to your work surface. For the eyes, drill two $^9/_{64}$ in. holes about 2 cm ($^3/_4$ in.) apart, about 5 cm (2 in.) from the rim.

2 Screw a beveled washer onto one $^1/_2$ in. bolt and a flat washer onto the other $^1/_2$ in. bolt.

3 Use the screwdriver to screw the bolts through the eye holes. Screw a locknut onto each bolt (see page 10).

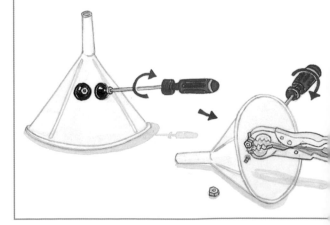

You will need

- 250 mL (8 oz.) plastic funnel
- two black beveled plumbing washers
- a black flat plumbing washer
- two $^1/_2$ in. bolts and locknuts
- a plastic-coated red screw hook
- 900 mL (30 oz.) plastic bottle • two 6-32 locknuts
- three 23 cm (9 in.) lengths of $^1/_4$ in. dowel
- 75 cm (30 in.) length of   • 3 in. eyelet bolt
  16 gauge red stranded wire
- two black beads that fit on the stranded wire
- pencil, ruler, one red and one black permanent marker
- work gloves and safety glasses
- C-clamps; hand drill with a $^7/_{64}$ in. bit, a $^9/_{64}$ in. bit, a $^1/_4$ in. bit and a $^1/_2$ in. bit; screwdriver; locking pliers

4 For the nose, drill a $7/64$ in. hole in the funnel, centered below the eyes. Screw in the red hook. Then screw the two 6-32 locknuts onto the screw end of the hook (see page 10).

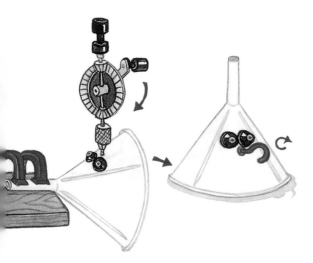

5 Clamp the bottle and drill three pairs of $1/4$ in. perch holes. Drill the first two holes opposite each other, about 5 cm (2 in.) from the bottom of the bottle.

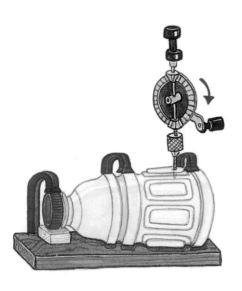

6 Drill the second pair of $1/4$ in. holes opposite each other, about 1 cm ($1/2$ in.) higher than the first set and about 5 cm (2 in.) to the side.

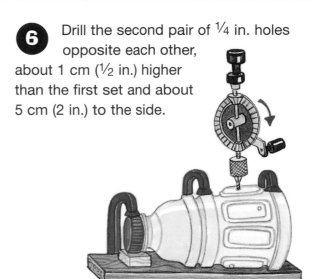

7 Drill the third pair of $1/4$ in. holes opposite each other, about 6 cm ($2 1/2$ in.) from the top of the bottle.

8 For the perches, color red and black stripes on the dowels with the markers.

9 Insert a dowel through each pair of perch holes, as shown.

10 If you are using thistle seeds, clamp the bottle and drill ⁹⁄₆₄ in. feeding holes about 2.5 cm (1 in.) above and below each perch. If you are using sunflower seeds, drill ¹⁄₂ in. feeding holes about 2.5 cm (1 in.) above and beside each perch.

11 Drill two ⁹⁄₆₄ in. holes opposite each other, about 2 cm (³⁄₄ in.) from the bottom of the bottle. Center the holes in between the perches, as shown.

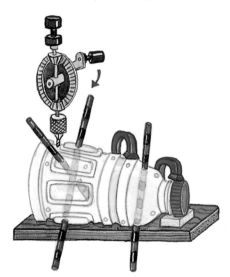

12 Poke the red wire in one hole and out the other. Pull it through until the ends are even.

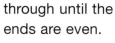

13 Thread the wire ends through a beveled washer. Twist the wires together for about 8 cm (3 in.), as shown.

14 To attach the head, poke the wire up through the funnel neck, as shown.

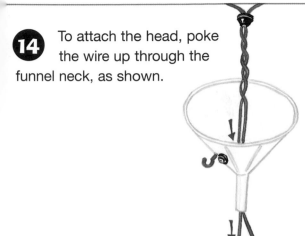

17 Unscrew the bottle top to fill the fly with seeds.

15 Unscrew the nut from the eyelet bolt. Push the bolt down through the neck of the funnel. Screw the nut back onto the bolt tightly, inside the funnel.

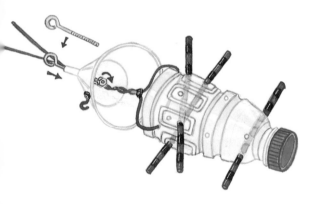

Other idea

• Decorate with electrical or reflective tape.

16 Curl the wire ends like antennae and slip a bead on each. Bend the wire ends to hold the beads.

Long-nosed, big-eyed bottle bug

Birds will go bug-eyed over this giant insect.

You will need

- six metal washers: two $9/16$, two $7/16$, two $5/16$
- red and yellow safety or automotive tape
- two black flat plumbing washers
- two lengths of 20 gauge galvanized wire: one 14 cm (5½ in.) and one 50 cm (20 in.)
- three ¾ in. bolts and locknuts
- a long-necked plastic ketchup bottle
- a brass door-stopper spring
- two lengths of 14 or 16 gauge black stranded wire: one 60 cm (24 in.) and one 75 cm (30 in.)

- six 25 cm (10 in.) lengths of 12 gauge black stranded wire
- six orange wire nuts
- pencil, scissors, ruler
- work gloves and safety glasses
- locking pliers; screwdriver; wire cutters; C-clamps; hand drill with a $5/32$ in. bit, a ¼ in. bit and a ½ in. bit; wire stripper or utility knife

1 For the eyes, place the two 9/16 metal washers on the red tape and trace around them. Cut out the circles with scissors. Stick a circle onto each washer. Make a small hole in the center with the tip of the scissors.

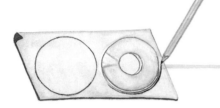

2 Slip a black washer onto a bolt. Add a 7/16 washer and then one of the red washers (from step 1). Repeat for the other eye.

3 Wind one end of the 14 cm (5½ in.) galvanized wire around the bolt of one eye twice and then slip on a 5/16 metal washer. Screw the locknut tightly onto the bolt (see page 10).

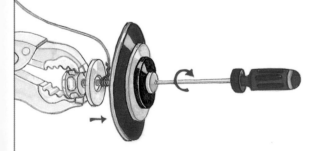

4 Repeat step 3 for the other eye so the eyes are connected by the galvanized wire.

5 For the nose, carefully cut the flip top off the bottle cap using the wire cutters. Poke a bolt through the metal disk of the door-stopper spring and then through the hole in the bottle cap, as shown. Screw the locknut onto the bolt (see page 10).

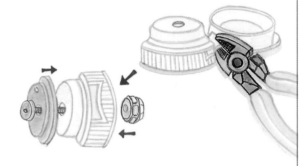

6 Poke the end of the door-stopper spring through the disk's hole and turn it so that it holds.

7 Push the wide end of the spring down to make a gap and slip in the wire that holds the eyes together. Slide it around the spring once so that the wire is caught in the spring. Twist the wire to hold it in place.

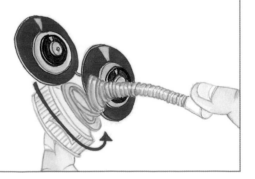

8 Push the nose down again to make a gap next to the wire and slip the eyes into the space.

9 Clamp the bottle to your work surface. Drill eight 5/32 in. drainage holes into one narrow side, as shown. This will be the stomach of the bug.

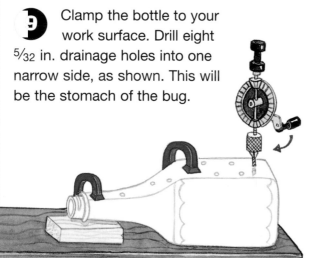

10 Drill three pairs of 1/4 in. perch holes about 5 cm (2 in.) apart on the wide sides of the bottle, as shown. The holes of each pair should be opposite each other.

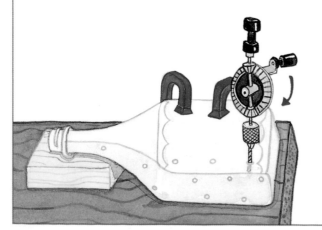

11 Drill about ten 1/2 in. feeding holes at different heights on the wide sides of the bottle, as shown.

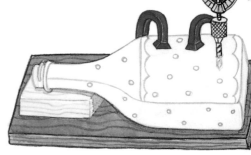

12 For the antennae, drill two 5/32 in. holes about 2 cm (3/4 in.) apart on the top of the neck and another two oppostie on the bottom.

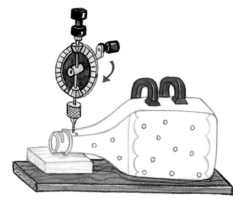

13 Bend the 60 cm (24 in.) black wire in half and poke the ends up through the neck holes, as shown. Make a knot near the top of the bottle, then curl the ends.

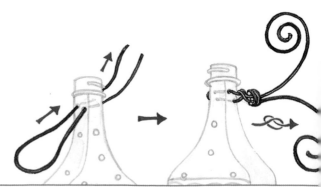

14 For the tail, use the 75 cm (30 in.) black wire and repeat steps 12 and 13, drilling the holes near the base of the bottle.

15 For each perch (the legs), twist two 25 cm (10 in.) black wires together. Poke them through each set of perch holes.

16 Ask an adult to carefully strip 1 cm (½ in.) of the plastic coating from the end of each perch using a wire stripper or a utility knife.

17 Screw a wire nut tightly onto each of the stripped ends. Bend the feet up.

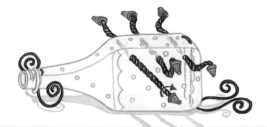

18 Decorate the bottle and the tip of the nose with strips of colored tape.

19 For hanging, slip one end of the long galvanized wire through the knot at the base of the antennae. Twist the wire so that it holds. Slip the other end of the wire through the tail's knot. Twist it to hold.

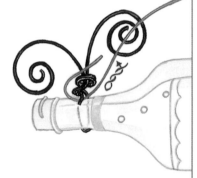

20 Fill the bottle with sunflower seeds or mixed seeds, then screw on the head. Hold the bug by the wire and, where the wire bends, twist it around a pencil to make a small loop.

Bird dog

One hot dog all dressed to go.

You will need

- 30 cm (12 in.) long log, 8–10 cm (3–4 in.) diameter
- 13 cm (5 in.) long log, about 6 cm (2½ in.) diameter
- four black beveled plumbing washers
- two ⁷⁄₁₆ metal washers
- round head screws: two 1 in., one 1½ in.
- two 3 in. square bend screw hooks
- 4 in. mending brace
- four 1½ in. flat head screws
- two metal rings
- 4 in. screw eyelet
- a branch, 40 cm (16 in.) long and about 2.5 cm (1 in.) diameter

- four 2 in. common nails
- 70 cm (28 in.) length of 16 gauge galvanized wire
- yellow or light-colored pencil and ruler
- work gloves and safety glasses
- bench vise or C-clamps; power drill with a 1 in. spade bit and a ¾ in. spade bit; hand drill with a ⅛ in. bit and a ³⁄₁₆ in. bit; screwdriver; pliers; saw; hammer

1 For the body, clamp the 30 cm (12 in.) log securely to your work surface. Ask an adult to use the power drill and both spade bits to drill 15 to 20 holes, about 2 cm (¾ in.) deep, all around the log.

For the head, clamp the 13 cm (5 in.) log securely. Ask an adult to use the power drill and both spade bits to drill six holes around the log.

For the eyes, clamp the head. Mark and drill two ⅛ in. pilot holes on the top of the head, about 2 cm (¾ in.) apart and about 5 cm (2 in.) from one end.

4 Slip a plumbing washer and a metal washer onto a 1 in. screw. Screw it into one of the pilot holes. Repeat for the other eye.

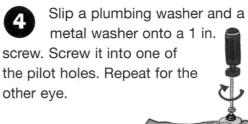

5 For the nose, drill a ⅛ in. pilot hole near the other end of the head. Slip two plumbing washers, flat sides together, onto the 1½ in. round head screw and screw it in.

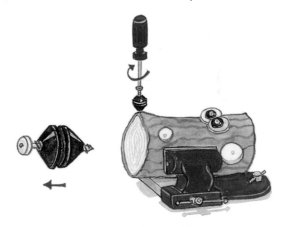

6 For the ears, drill two ³⁄₁₆ in. holes, about 4 cm (1½ in.) apart, near the back of the head. Use pliers to screw the screw hooks in the holes.

7 To attach the head to the body, place half of the mending brace on the bottom of the head, as shown. Mark the brace holes with the colored pencil. Remove the brace. Clamp the head and drill ⅛ in. pilot holes where marked.

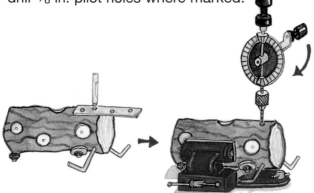

8 Screw the mending brace to the head with the flat head screws.

9 Place the free half of the mending brace on top of the body, as shown. Mark the holes with the colored pencil. Remove the brace. Clamp the body and drill ⅛ in. pilot holes where marked.

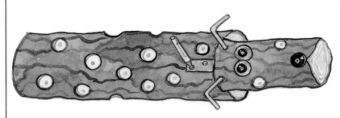

10 Slip a metal ring onto the brace. Ask a helper to hold the head in place and screw the brace to the body.

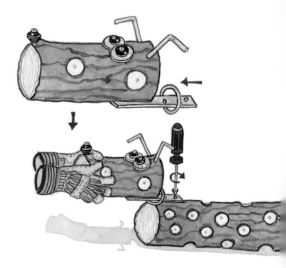

11 For the tail, drill a ³⁄₁₆ in. pilot hole about 2 cm (¾ in.) from the back of the body. Screw in the screw eyelet using the pliers.

12 For the legs, clamp the 40 cm (16 in.) branch and saw it into four 10 cm (4 in.) pieces.

13 One at a time, drill a ⅛ in. pilot hole about 1 cm (½ in.) from one end of each leg. Nail the legs to the body.

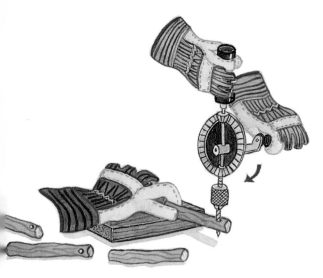

14 For hanging, wind one end of the wire around the neck ring. Slip the wire through a metal ring. Wind the other end of the wire around the eyelet tail.

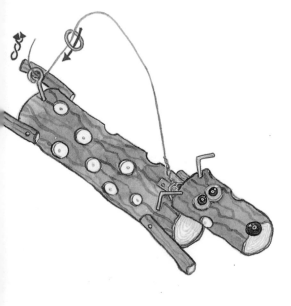

15 Hold the dog up by the ring. Where the wire bends, turn the ring a couple of times to twist the wire and hold the ring in place.

16 Fill the holes with peanut butter, suet and/or even old cheese.

Other idea

- Make a flying reindeer by adding antlers and a red nose and painting on hooves.

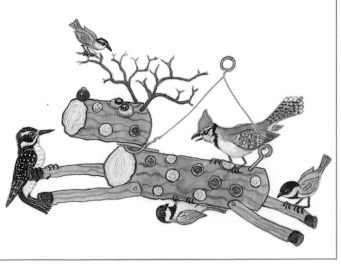

Fat cat

A cat birds will love ... to peck at!

You will need

- a pack of suet, 11 cm (4½ in.) square
- 1 x 8 pine board, 25 cm (10 in.) long
- 1 x 2 pine board, 23 cm (9 in.) long
- ¾ in. half-round molding: two 11 cm (4½ in.) lengths, one 18 cm (7 in.) length
- six ¾ in. finishing nails
- 14 or 16 gauge covered stranded wire: red: 2.3 m (7½ ft.); green: 2.4 m (8 ft.); blue: 90 cm (3 ft.)
- two black beveled plumbing washers
- two ⅜ metal washers
- two ¾ in. round head screws
- a small plastic screw top (from juice cartons or bottles)
- 1 in. round head screw
- a red wire nut
- ¾ in. brass hinge and screws
- 1½ in. brass hook and eye
- two brass screw eyes
- 45 cm (18 in.) length of brass wire
- pencil, ruler, exterior wood glue and rag
- work gloves and safety glasses
- C-clamps, coping saw, hammer, hand drill with a ⁹⁄₆₄ in. bit and a ³⁄₃₂ bit, wire cutters, screwdriver, pliers

1 Place the suet on the larger board so that one edge is even with the bottom. Trace around it with a pencil, then put it aside.

1 Clamp the board to your work surface. Using the coping saw, cut along the pencil line (see page 9). Check that the suet fits easily in the opening.

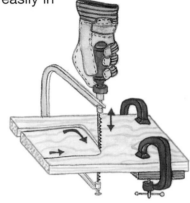

2 Spread glue on the flat side of the 11 cm (4½ in.) molding pieces. Nail the molding to the sides of the opening using a finishing nail at each end. Wipe off excess glue.

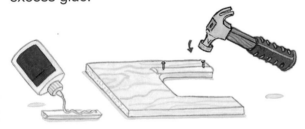

4 Beside both pieces of molding, mark five X's down the board about 2 cm (¾ in.) apart.

5 Mark four X's on the molding pieces so they are in between the X's from step 4.

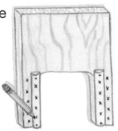

6 Clamp the board and drill ⁹/₆₄ in. holes all the way through each X.

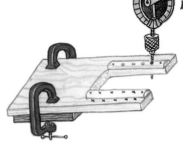

7 Spread glue on the flat side of the 18 cm (7 in.) molding piece. Nail it to the top of the board using a finishing nail at each end. Wipe off excess glue.

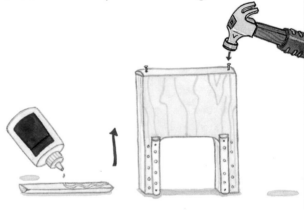

8 For the ears, mark X's on the top molding. Measuring from one edge, make an X at 1 cm (½ in.), another at 2.5 cm (1 in.), the next at 4.5 cm (1¾ in.) and the last at 6 cm (2½ in.). Repeat from the other edge. Drill a ⁹/₆₄ in. hole into each X, about 2.5 cm (1 in.) deep.

9 Use the wire cutters to carefully cut two 10 cm (4 in.) lengths of red wire and two 15 cm (6 in.) lengths of green wire.

10 Bend the wires in half. Dab a bit of glue into the ear holes and poke the wire ends into the holes, as shown. Wipe off excess glue.

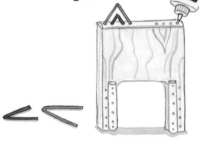

11 For the eyes, mark and drill two $^3/_{32}$ in. pilot holes about 3.5 cm ($1^3/_8$ in.) from the top edge, about 2.5 cm (1 in.) apart. Slip a black plumbing washer and a metal washer onto each $^3/_4$ in. screw. Screw the eyes into the board.

12 For the nose, ask an adult to hold the plastic top. Carefully drill a $^9/_{64}$ in. hole in the center. Drill two holes on each side of the top for the whiskers.

13 Use the wire cutters to carefully cut two 15 cm (6 in.) lengths of blue wire. Poke them through the holes in the side of the top, as shown.

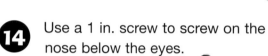

14 Use a 1 in. screw to screw on the nose below the eyes.

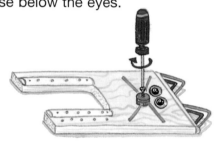

15 For the stomach, lace a 2 m (80 in.) length of green wire through the holes in the molding, crisscrossing it like a shoelace. Lace a 2 m (80 in.) length of red wire the same way through the outer holes.

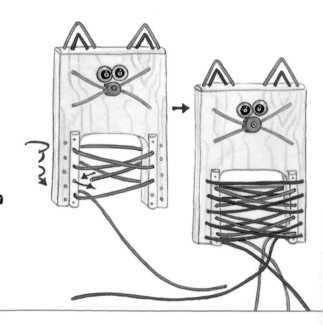

16 Knot the wires together at the back, as shown. Twist them together and cut the ends even with the wire cutters. Screw the wire nut onto the ends.

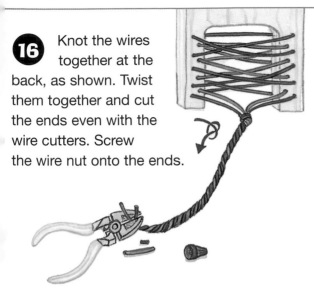

17 For the toes, mark and drill three ⁹⁄₆₄ in. holes into the edge of the small board near each end, about 1 cm (½ in.) apart, as shown.

18 Use the wire cutters to carefully cut six 10 cm (4 in.) lengths of blue wire. Dab a bit of glue into the holes, and poke the wires into the holes. Bend the tips under with pliers. Wipe off excess glue.

19 Place the hinge on the outer edge of the bottom left corner of the cat, as shown. Screw it in place.

20 Center the cat on the small board. Screw the other half of the hinge into the board.

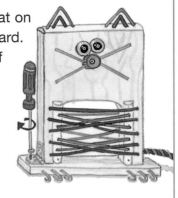

21 Screw the brass hook into the other edge of the cat, about 4.5 cm (1¾ in.) from the bottom. Screw the eye into the small board about 1 cm (½ in.) from the edge. Check that the hook fits into the eye. You can adjust it by unscrewing the eye slightly.

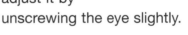

22 Place the suet in the cat's stomach, and fasten the hook and eye. For hanging, screw a screw eye into each side, about 3 cm (1¼ in.) from the top. Twist an end of the wire to each screw eye.

Three-footed booby

This strange visitor will attract a lot of attention.

You will need

- 6 m (7 yds.) 12 gauge blue unstranded wire
- a tomato cage, about 1 m (1 yd.) high
- 3 in. wall scraper with a handle
- two 2 in. eyelet bolts and nuts
- two black flat plumbing washers
- metal washers: two $7/16$, two $5/16$, one $1/4$
- two $3/4$ in. bolts and locknuts
- 50 cm (20 in.) length of a $5/8$ in. dowel
- 1 in. screw
- 18 gauge coated or galvanized wire: six 15 cm (6 in.) lengths, two 35 cm (14 in.) lengths
- 12 gauge red stranded wire: 150 cm (60 in.)
- two plastic flowerpot saucers: one about 25 cm (10 in.) and one about 30 cm (12 in.) diameter
- pencil and ruler
- work gloves and safety glasses
- wire cutters; needlenose pliers; C-clamps; hand drill with a $5/32$ in. bit, a $3/32$ in. bit and a $1/4$ in. bit; a screwdriver; locking pliers; coping saw

1 For one foot, carefully cut a 70 cm (28 in.) length of blue wire. Bend it 10 cm (4 in.) from one end. Bend the wire four more times, every 6 cm (2½ in.), as shown.

2 Use the needlenose pliers to squeeze each bend tighter.

3 Wind the short end of the wire around the long end, as shown.

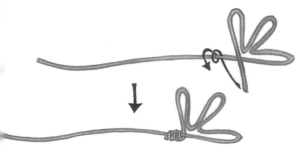

4 Bend the long wire up and wind it around one leg of the tomato cage. Wind the end around the bottom ring to hold the foot in place.

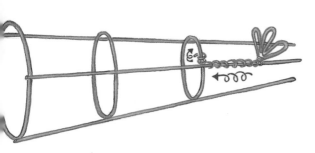

5 Repeat steps 1 to 4 for the other two feet.

6 For the eyes, clamp the wall scraper to your work surface. Drill two $^5/_{32}$ in. holes into the handle, about 2.5 cm (1 in.) up from the scraper part.

7 Screw an eyelet bolt into each hole in the handle. Screw a nut onto the end of each bolt.

8 For each eye, slip a black plumbing washer followed by a $^7/_{16}$ metal washer onto a bolt. Poke the bolt through an eyelet bolt, then slip on a $^5/_{16}$ metal washer. Screw a locknut onto the bolt (see page 10).

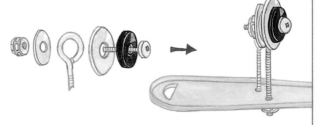

9 Clamp the dowel and cut one end at an angle. Drill a $^3/_{32}$ in. hole into this end, as shown.

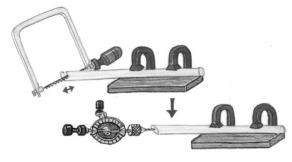

10 Drill another two holes through the dowel, one 30 cm (12 in.) and the other 8 cm (3 in.) from the flat end.

11 Clamp the scraper and drill a ³/₃₂ in. hole, about 2.5 cm (1 in.) from the end of the handle.

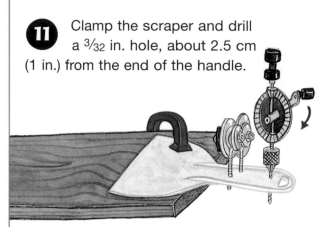

12 Slip the ¼ washer onto the 1 in. screw and screw the scraper into the hole on the top of the dowel (from step 9), as shown.

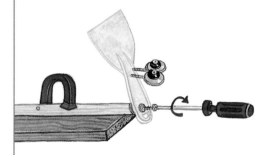

13 To attach the dowel to the cage, poke one end of a 35 cm (14 in.) length of 18 gauge wire through one hole from step 10. Wind the wire around the dowel and the tomato cage ring. Twist the wire ends together. Repeat for the other hole.

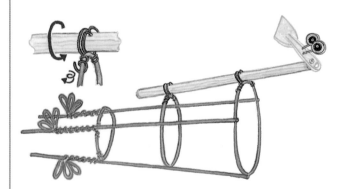

14 To make the head feathers, carefully cut a 90 cm (35 in.) length of blue wire. Start by winding one end of the wire around the top ring of the cage and keep winding up around the dowel. Poke it up through the opening in the scraper handle and curl the end.

15 Make other head feathers using different colors and lengths of wire and repeating step 14. Or just wind wire around the top of the dowel and around the handle.

16 To make tail feathers, carefully cut a 60 cm (24 in.) length of blue wire and bend it in half. Catch the bend on the cage leg opposite the head, as shown, and wind the wires once around the top ring. Curl the ends. Repeat for other feathers using different lengths of wire.

17 To attach the feed saucers, bend a 15 cm (6 in.) length of 18 gauge wire in half. Wind the ends around the top ring of the cage where a leg meets the ring. Repeat at all the leg joints around the top ring and the middle ring.

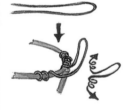

18 Place each saucer in the ring it fits and mark on its rim where the leg joints are. Clamp each saucer and drill 5/32 in. holes on the marks.

19 Drill eight 5/32 in. drainage holes into the bottom of each saucer.

20 Place the saucers in the rings, lining the holes up with the leg joints. Slip the wire loops from step 17 through the holes and bend them to hold the saucers in place. Fill the saucers with seeds.

Other idea

- To make this a bird bath, don't drill the drainage holes in step 19.

Chicken delight

Enough seeds to feed a big brood.

You will need

- an old metal tablespoon
- a garden claw
- ¾ in. steel cable strap
- two 1½ in. screws
- six 1¼ in. red plastic-coated screw hooks
- an armful of thin branches or twigs and garden pruners
- about one hundred 1 in. common nails
- exterior glue and toothpick • pencil and ruler
- work gloves and safety glasses
- needlenose pliers, screwdriver, C-clamps, hand drill with a ³⁄₃₂ in. bit and a ¹⁄₁₆ in. bit, hammer

- ¾ in. hose clamp
- ¼ in. wire rope clip
- 2 x 8 pine board, 23 cm (9 in.) long

1 For the beak, hold the spoon near the neck with the pliers and bend the handle up, as shown.

2 Slide the hose clamp ring onto the handle of the garden claw, just below the prongs. Slip the spoon in the ring, as shown. Tighten the screw on the ring with a screwdriver to hold everything in place.

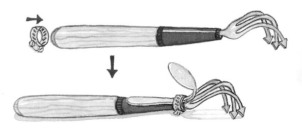

3 For the eyes, loosen the nuts on the wire rope clip. Slip it onto the middle prong of the claw and slide it on until it sits just above the spoon.

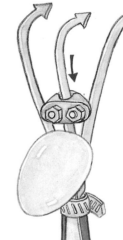

4 Use a toothpick to dab a bit of glue on the threads of the rope clip bolt, as shown. Screw the nuts back on tightly with the pliers. Let dry.

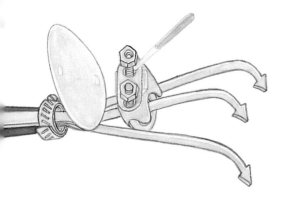

5 Put the cable strap on one side of the board and mark the holes with a pencil. Clamp the board to your work surface and drill $3/32$ in. pilot holes where marked.

6 Use the $1\frac{1}{2}$ in. screws to screw the cable strap and claw to the board.

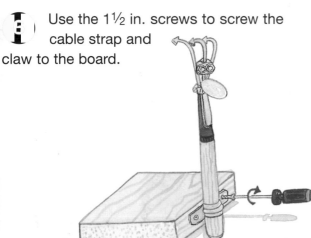

7 For the toes, screw three red hooks into the board on each side of the claw handle. Make the middle toe a bit higher than the other two.

8 Use garden pruners to carefully cut the branches into about one hundred 10 cm to 15 cm (4 in. to 6 in.) lengths. Also cut three 40 cm (16 in.) lengths for the tail.

9 Drill ¹⁄₁₆ in. pilot holes about 1 cm (½ in.) from one end of the branches. Clamp the branches or have someone hold them while you drill.

10 Nail the shorter branches around all four sides of the board as tightly together as possible. (It is easier if you unscrew the toes, nail the branches beside the screw holes and then screw the toes back in.)

11 For the tail, nail the three long branches to the back.

12 Fill with sunflower seeds or mixed seeds.

Bird food

Your feeder will attract different kinds of birds depending on what you fill it with. Here is a list of some favorite bird foods. You can either buy bags of seeds at the grocery store or make your own mixes.

Sunflower seeds: Black or striped seeds are popular with nearly all birds.

Mixed seeds: Choose a bag that has mostly sunflower seeds, millet and corn, because that is what the birds pick out and eat — the other seeds are often just wasted!

Thistle seeds: A favorite food for finches.

Suet: A fat that is great for birds during the winter.

Peanuts: Make sure you buy unsalted peanut pieces.

Unsalted peanut butter: Mix it with corn meal for a better bird snack.

Fruits: Apples, oranges, raisins and currants make a different treat.

Many birds will feed wherever the feeder is placed, but some birds have preferences. Some, such as goldfinches, purple finches and cardinals, like hanging feeders filled with seeds. Hanging suet is a favorite treat in the winter for nearly all birds, especially woodpeckers, nuthatches and blue jays. Other birds, like grosbeaks and finches, prefer trays, and some, such as juncos, sparrows and mourning doves, will only eat on the ground! Chickadees happily feed just about anywhere. To attract all sorts of birds, put feeders at different heights and fill them with different kinds of bird food.